I0159318

Printed in the United States of America

CA Morrison Publishing, 2017

ISBN 978-0999612804

CA Morrison Publishing
2600 Smoky Topaz Ln
Raleigh, NC 27610

www.courtlandmorrison.com

Introduction

Welcome to my literary debut. .I hope you can feel my excitement and joy in poetry. Writing from my heart, mind, and soul to you.

I want to say thank you to everyone who has supported me as I begin this new journey.

First Steps

My first visual, my first listen, my first touch

The sense of sight, sense of hearing, sense of dexterity and feel

These steps as a toddler, to child , from child to teenager, to

Adulthood

Yet as we grow older we regress back to a toddler state

First steps is how we learn , grow , and experience for a lifetime

Tender fingers, brain like a sponge asorbing this new

knowledge

Shaping the future and making new paths for a journey that has

Already been established

First steps remembering past thoughts and correlated meanings

Good and bad experiences a process of a lifetime of learning

These beginning steps an artifact embedded in our minds forever

First Steps

Inspirational

Extend my mind

To extend my mind, I must dream and set
my expectations high.
I must contour my eyes to see past the sun
but into a whole new cosmos.
I must breathe deeply and expand my lungs
let the oxygen matriculate into them. Like
reading a book expand my knowledge base
and capture a new vocabulary.
Let my heart not sorrow from the but bleed
for the future.
Extend my mind and dream and my
thoughts flow and flow. Dream on and let
my talents fruition to my anointed future.
To extend my mind...

I arise

I have a belief in my mind I can do all things

My path is set each of my steps are
measured again and again

I humble myself, but I study opinions with a
sterile stare

Attentive mind selective tongue

From when I speak it's deliberate but
concise

I walk with strength upright and passion

I listen intently with an open heart

Desires is always shown in mine eyes

Compassion comes from my heart

Humility comes from my soul

I arise

These beliefs are the basis of my character

My written integrity of honor

Pouring out of my soul

I arise

My Era of time

My era of time a true case of revolving
hands of time

Revolving but not in a way we want it to go

Mistrust, hatred, violence, discourse

What happen to love, unity, trust, and
charity

It was washed away like the tide of the
ocean

Now its dark vengeful death sings its tune
daily

I look to the sky in the face of death
destruction and despair

I see glitters of light from the heavens that
shine through the cloud of darkness

The stars and moon show a glow

However from the East is the rising of the
sun

The sun with no effort at all opens the sky to its majesty

Darkness can only hide but can never defeat the aura of the sun

Like the sun we all have aura that can be a beacon of light

The righteous know this beacon of light as Jesus Christ

For he is the light of the world

His glow, aura is unimaginable

This era of destruction and negativity can be turned if we only believe and have faith in him

Lets take back our era of time

Lets fulfill what its suppose to be

A era of love, peace, charity, unity, and compassion

My era, your era, Our era of time

A New Horizon

A new beginning, a new horizon is set into me

I must remove these old ragged thoughts from me

A new institution a new fire is formed

One to bring new ideals to bare and opportunities to seek

My new horizon is a mold from past experiences that many can relate

I emulate my father for he has set my path and work ethics

My mother to seek what I desire but maintain civility

A new beginning, a new horizon is set in stone

Like a new book just waiting for the first pages to be turned

The dawning of a new tomorrow the beginning of a new future

A play on words which is so useful

A new horizon what a way to begin

I see this journey will not be easy

Through trials and tribulations there will be

Knowing from the past going forward the experiences will be needed

It will help me guide instinctively through those times of bare

A new beginning, A new horizon

I am ready to go

Seek the standard, be the standard, exceed the standard

This is the new horizon I shall go

Inspiration

My family my friends

my brother and sister in arms

my inspiration

So many people who have mentored me,
believe in me, love me

So many who took me by the hand and said
you can do it

don't doubt yourself, be your own man, set
the world on fire

my inspiration

I use my poetry, my words, to set the pace,
put the world on notice

there is a light that shines bright. A light that
glows luminescent through out

the shadows. I set an institution in my heart
to inspire.

I inspire the children that hard work, faith, and determination will make you strong

character traits to be a leader, be distinguished, be humble, work diligently.

My inspiration my family, my friends

Not a day goes by that your influence does not strengthen me

So many ways to say so many thoughts I convey

My family, my friends you inspire me every day.

Religious

Power of the Tongue Voice of the Almighty

I shine I thrive I innovate you set my mind ablaze, yet your heart is divine you set me free to breathe I feel the consulate of your mind which brings respect peace and love write with passion penmanship is boldness set my mind free from the pain of the world.

Free from the hands of the angered young man or the cries of the lonely girl. Lost to the concept of reality tv yet their talents are hidden to hold on this ride of the in-crowd's roller coaster ride risen and, yet they remain silent. Instead of letting their light shine or unmask the skills within that have so far been blinded...talk to me

Talk to me and see the glory that is deeply
divine natural and powerful it burns hotter
than the surface of the sun yet colder than
the arctic circle taller than the Himalayas it's
my profound voice that booms and shakes
the ground makes nature be obedient yet
calms me like summer breeze coming off
the ocean young man young woman do not
be troubled for your true self is not of this
world show your strength and intellectual
ability for the concept of reality is happiness
in yourself

Love in yourself; success is in your hands so
don't let another define your wealth; and
don't be fooled by their games their body
language tells a lie, because their pockets
don't say the same. Yet our enemies will be
our foot stools; their pain our grace. for they
too had when it came down to it yet us real
ones keep our face...

The evil knows not what they afford. They
give me desire to push through the most

turbulent times the love of thine self-molds
me shapes me provokes me an intuition of
fire that glows upon my enemy's. I am not
fooled but delighted in being to speak with
the absence of profane and explicitly
segregate my words to a few. Give glory to
the most high show the faith of walking not
by sight is the most I need.

For I need thee oh Lord for in you I trust and
believe. while the enemy seeks to devour,
your love God is my safety my soul you
keep. I will press toward the mark for
chosen is I. That I shall stand the test and
real the harvest of many blessing bestowed
upon me from high.

The blessings he gives are so many I bow
down on my knees to give him the most
praise. Knowing he gave me shelter, food,
clothing and ability to breathe in I am
forever grateful I know when I am down
never to look around for the angels surround

me to protect me for no weapon formed against me shall prosper.

...and any tongue rising against me in judgement shall be condemned; for they boast and think highly of themselves still they'll never sit higher than him. Poses the power, orchestrate the hours and still have time to provide his grace like him

For he is the lord of lords and king of kings the alpha and the omega the beginning and the end. He is the light the light that all shall see when the trumpet sounds. Oh, what a feeling of joy.

Courtland Morrison & Erica Stillwell

My Soul

My soul is yours, from the pale moonlit
night sky

to the stillness of the lake on a mid-summer
nights eve

My soul is indebted to you from beginning
to end

My soul is given under your name

From the horrid acts of vengeance and
unmanly cruelty

My soul is indebted to you from beginning
to end

My soul is known throughout existence

You created my soul through the greatness
of your name

Your individual philosophies and unique
concepts

Keep my soul indebted to you from
beginning to end

My soul is yours, you said do not fear, do not struggle

yet bring all your burdens upon you

For you bestow all the many blessings on us

For my Lord and Savior Jesus Christ

My soul is indebted to you always,

My Soul

My Blessings

My blessings are many his love is so true

What a privilege to raise my hands to my
Lord in prayer

The cornerstone of my heart blessing to my
soul

I exalt my father in heaven

Giving me breath in my lungs, clothing to
cover me, shelter from the weather

I lift his name the most high to this day

He fills with me passion, love, and
endearment

He blessed me with this talent of poetry

To match emotions to words, love and grace

I am fortunate to have this and thank the
most high every day for this gift

His blessings so numerous in the mind's eye
its too hard to fathom

My friends my family whom I cherish and respect

The Lord Jesus Christ who I bow and worship to

He is the truth and way of the light the Alpha and Omega

Beginning and the End

I fall on my knees every night and give thanks

I praise him and love him

Jesus Christ my father heaven I give thee o lord

May you continue to bless me, my friends, my family

and they do the same

My blessings so many, his love infinite

I exalt you my father

Amen

Relationships

Together Forever

My love my lady the one who brings
purpose to my life
Her sweet smile and soulful touch spans my
horizon
I feel her presence when I look into a mirror
She is so great in so many ways

She awakens me with a kiss on the cheek
She knows how to soothe me from times of
discomfort
Yet she controls my anger and aggression
Her love for me is fondness my love for her
is forever

Together Forever is my heart that she
possesses the key
Her love my love is endless which we share
together
Boundless love mutual affection we grow
stronger everyday

Together Forever
My love is intimate only on you
To you I am forever in love with you

Without you I'm lost

From the first time met you, I knew you
were the one for me
Your soft brown eyes, and humble smile
drew me
Yet your gentle touch, sweet attitude kept
me

For our time together has been wild and
wonderous
You always knew how to talk to me in
troubled times,
keep my faith in heavenly times, show me
my strength
in weakness of times

You always stayed in my corner and
nurtured me to be stronger
in times of separation
Yet I know our bond is strong and only gets
stronger everyday

without you I feel lost, but I know in my
heart
your just moment away.

My Reflections

The shining of the sun during the day, the
gaze of the moon at night
Are just a reflection of my thoughts I carry
everyday
The sun so bright that is seen everywhere,
and the heat it projects energizes my mind
my emotions to the physical beats of my
heart.
The moon just like the sun is seen but
pushes in and outward flow of the oceans
from low to
high tide this balances my wakeup to
slumber, so peaceful to sleep and rest one's
body from
a day of labor
The surface of water how it reflects the sun
and the moon, from just a sliver to full
abundance

is like a mirror that shows our face as we
grow from infant to adulthood
So many reflections so many insights how
we reflect nature and nature reflects us
Reflections just like the ancient hands of
time we continue evolve and change over
time
My reflection, your reflection a tide of hope
and passion that we reflect upon each other
My reflections

One Wish for one more day
My time is minimum, my love is forever
From the depths of the oceans to the peaks
of the Himalayas
For I only wish to be with you one more day
One day in my life, is thirst to my soul
From the crown on your head to the soles of
your feet
For I only wish to be with you one more day
Your love brings me to my feet, Like the sun
rising on a new Sunday
Perception and understanding are your main
attributes
For I only wish to be with you one more day
The slight coolness of the night sends
shivers down my spine just thinking of you
You mesmerize my intellect, which
sequences the thirst of my soul
For I only wish to be with you one more day
My time is minimum, my lover is forever
From the depths of the oceans to the peaks
of the Himalayas

For I only wish to be with you one more day
To keep my trust in your eyes, keep you
calm in troubled times
Keep doubt from streaming through your
mind
For my love will never leave you, one day of
silence means nothing to me
For my wish will be fulfilled one more day
One more day

The Joy of love
My joy of love I see in your eyes
Your soft voice innocent laugh makes me
smile
For your in my heart
I can feel that one kiss that is my gateway to
your soul
Your soft hands and delicate eyes serves as
my promise to be with you
I will bring trust, honor, chivalry to our
relationship
One second, one minute, one hour, one day
We will build our relationship together
I can see a future that we share together
My love for you your love for me will grow
From innocent conversations to detailed
narratives
My joys of love are beginning
Will you join me????

Tear in the sand

I walk along a beach with a tear in my eye
with the loss of my love drawn from me
My love for her was priceless
Her beauty brought me to my knees
The gentle voice and flow of words
consumed me
Her spirit is mind blowing, which threw me
into a
state of confusion
She touched my heart with her sensual
beauty
She destroyed me with her sexual brevity
I was her physical puppet which she
controlled
with her mental strings
Alas my love for her, her love for me faded
Now I walk alone this beach with a tear in
my eye
Waiting for the next best thing in my own
Iniquity

The day I will always remember
It was a special day I remember
I was in the bookstore looking for recipes to
try
Then by faith maybe destiny I caught eyes
with you
Your eyes brought a sense of peace I had
never felt
Your voice so sweet and subtle a soliloquy
to my mind
You came to where I was standing asking
me if need help with anything
I was puzzled I was at a lost for words for a
second
I then said I was looking for a recipe book
She shown me different ones till I found the
right one
I told her thank you for the assistance
I left the bookstore but my mind was telling
me ask her
For this might be someone who changes
your world
I go back into the bookstore and see her
again

She says hey back so soon was there
something else
I can help you with
I tell her yes but it's something more
personal
She looks at me puzzled but says she can try
I tell her there is a young lady I would like
get to know her but I am not sure how to
approach her
She says be yourself and be honest at all
times
She said I hope that helps I said very much
I told her thank you for giving me
confirmation on knowing that I have been
watching you from afar that I always wanted
to talk to you
She looked at me and I can see the blush on
her cheeks and slight tear in her eye
She was taken back but said to me in
sincerity you are truly unique and know one
has approached me in this form and fashion.
We exchanged numbers and went on
This day I always replay for it was the
beginning of our lives together

Bonus

There is something in you young man feed
it.

I will feed it and harvest it, like a farmer
takes heed to their crop it must be well taken
care of.

 I must keep my faith and walk on a limb.

 For I know where my strength lies and how
my foundation is built.

For the harvest is the blessing of the Lord
and my glorification for his name sake.

He promotes me, he builds me, he
characterizes me,

I am only a insturment of his mighty vision
and voice

I continue to learn, to see and how to use
this blessing he has given me

So I must feed and nurture this gift of words
and written architecture

A young man, a poet, a student, a soldier

I will be like a rose and grow into maturity

A Poets Distinction

The art of my eye distinction of my mind
dedicated in one time

I see the glean of the sun, passing of the
sparrows overhead
The gushing of the wind is the Lords voice
getting my attention

I see the words that he wants me to see
I feel the strength of the Holy Ghost when
he consumes my mind

The constitution of words that's in the Bible
is my motivation
It shows my intellect which the Lord gave
Usage of words is my pride, passion, fervor

The art of my eye, distinction of my mind
dedicated in one time

Distinction is my character, Dedication is in
my heart
The art is my poetry, Chasing my destiny,
my dream
A Poets Distinction